Relating Jesus Pr…

List the names of 4-6 non-Christians in your circle of friends, family, co-workers, etc.

1. ______________________
2. ______________________
3. ______________________
4. ______________________
5. ______________________
6. ______________________

As you **PRAY** for them, consider…

- How can I **SERVE** them in practical ways?
- How can I **COOPERATE** with what the Holy Spirit is doing in their lives? How can I reach out together with other Christian friends.
- Do I **LISTEN** more than I talk? What are my friends' felt needs? Where are they on their spiritual journey?
- Am I ready to **SHARE** what Christ has done in my own life?
- Who might I **INVITE** to a group or church event where they can be exposed to Christ's message, power and love?

Check off each day that you pray, serve or spend significant time with individuals on your prayer list. There are additional prayer cards located in the back for future use.

Detach this card along perforation…

	1	2	3	4	5	6	7	8	9	10	11	12	13	14	15	16	17	18	19	20	21	22	23	24	25	26	27	28	29	30	31
January																															
February																														X	X
March																															
April																															X
May																															
June																															X
July																															
August																															
September																															X
October																															
November																															X
December																															

Detach this card along perforation…

Detach this card along perforation…

MY PRAYER LIST

1. _____
2. _____
3. _____
4. _____
5. _____
6. _____

Detach this card along perforation…

Relating Jesus Participant's Guide

Relating Jesus
Participant's Guide

Making Christ Real
in Your Everyday Relationships

Jim Egli

Cell Group Resources™ a division of TOUCH Outreach Ministries
Houston, TX, U.S.A.

Published by Cell Group Resources™
10055 Regal Row, Suite 180
Houston, TX 77040, U.S.A
(713) 896-7478 • Fax (713) 896-1874

Copyright © 2002 by Jim Egli

All rights reserved. No part of this publication may be reproduced, stored in a retrieval system, or transmitted, in any form or by any means, electronic, mechanical, photocopying, recording, or otherwise, without the prior written permission of the publisher. Printed in the United States of America.

Cover design by Don Bleyl
Text design by Brandy Egli
Editing by Brandy Egli

International Standard Book Number: 1-880828-46-4

All Scripture quotations, unless otherwise indicated, are from the Holy Bible, New Living Translation, Copyright © 1996 by the Tyndale Charitable Trust. Used with permission.

Cell Group Resources™ is a book-publishing division of TOUCH Outreach Ministries, a resource and consulting ministry for churches with a vision for cell-based local church structure.

For more information on other
Cell Group Resources or CellGroup Journal
Call 1-800-735-5865 or 713-896-7478
Find us on the World Wide Web at
http://www.cellgrouppeople.com

Table of Contents

Introduction 7

Lesson One — Pray 9

Lesson Two — Serve 13

Lesson Three — Cooperate 19

Lesson Four — Listen 23

Lesson Five — Share 27

Lesson Six — Invite 33

Notes 39

Introduction

Welcome to the *Relating Jesus* study. For the next six weeks or so, you and your fellow small group members will look at how to share Jesus' love and truth with people who don't yet know Him.

I am confident that you will enjoy the journey because of my own experience. About fifteen years ago, my wife, Vicki, and I concluded that loving others to Christ should be central to our lives. We haven't lived this principle perfectly, and we still have a lot to learn, but we have discovered that making Jesus real to others in many ways boils down to one word—"friendship."

Everyone needs good friends. And when you enter into meaningful friendships, you almost always receive more than you give. In the process of building these friendships, you will see others enter into the most wonderful relationship—friendship with Christ!

You will also discover that long before you build meaningful friendships with nonbelievers, the Holy Spirit has begun to work in their lives. You are not alone. You are working in partnership with God's Spirit and Christian teammates.

Giving and receiving friendship is a wonderful adventure, so enjoy it!

Jim Egli

Lesson One – Pray

How Do People Really Come to Christ?

1. What comes to your mind when you hear the word "evangelism?"

    ❏ Billy Graham ❏ Gospel tracts
    ❏ Caring friendships ❏ Talking
    ❏ Going door-to-door ❏ Listening
    ❏ Other: _____
    _____

2. Who was most influential in your decision to follow Christ? What was that person's relationship to you (friend, relative, co-worker, teacher, stranger, etc.)?

3. What did the person do that influenced you?

4. How many times did you hear the gospel before you came to Christ?

5. How long did the process take? How many people were involved in the process?

Evangelism: Myths & Realities

Usually, discussing answers to the above questions reveals four myths and realities about evangelism.

Myth #1: Evangelism means talking to strangers.
- The reality is that most people (80%) are reached by friends and family members.
- What does this mean? You are called to show God's love to those closest to you.

Myth #2: Evangelism means saying just the right words.
- The reality is that people are won to Christ through active love and words.
- What does this mean? You should serve others, pray for them, and take time to listen and care.

Myth #3: Conversion is normally instantaneous.
- The reality is that conversion is usually a process.
- What does this mean? You can relax and give people time.

Myth #4: People are brought to Christ through the influence of just one person.
- The reality is that the more Christians a nonbeliever knows, the more easily he or she will come to Christ.
- What does this mean? You should introduce your non-Christian friends to as many Christians as possible.

These realities are also reported in the Bible.

- People like Levi (Mark 2:13-15), Andrew (John 1:40-42a), Cornelius (Acts 10:19-33), Lydia (Acts 16:13-15), and the Philippian jailer (Acts 16:29-34) all brought their family members and friends to Christ.
- Jesus said, "one person plants and someone else harvests" (John 4:37), implying that evangelism is a process that takes time and involves multiple people playing different roles.

Who Do You Know that Needs Christ?

You are in a unique position to reach those closest to you. No one else has the same set of relationships that you do.

1. Who do you know that does not yet know Christ? Write down names of people in the following categories:

   Family members:

   Friends:

   Co-workers or classmates:

   Neighbors:

If you don't have any nonbelievers in your current circle of influence, think of the friends of your friends, or "steal" names from someone else in your group.

2. Write the names you listed above on your Relating Jesus Prayer Card.

3. Pray for these people as consistently as possible, asking God to make His love real to them through you.

Lesson Two – Serve

How's It Going?

In Lesson One, you learned that most Christians were influenced to receive Christ through friends or family members who prayed for them, loved them and communicated Christ to them. Last week, you were asked to pray consistently for those near you who do not yet know Christ. How did it go?

❏ Great! I prayed for them every day.
❏ Not bad. I prayed several days for them.
❏ Oops! I entirely forgot.
❏ Other answer or excuse: _____

Take time now to share your answer with someone near you and take a few moments to pray for your friends, relatives, and co-workers or classmates who do not yet know Christ. You can check today off your card.

What's Your Favorite Song?

What is one of your favorite songs? What first caught your attention—the song's music or its words?

Usually, people are first attracted to a song by its melody. Only later, often in a quiet moment, like when they are driving alone at night, do they notice the full meaning of its words.

That is also how communicating the good news of Christ works. Most people are drawn by the music—by the love, joy, or integrity—that they see in Christians' lives. Only after they have been attracted by the practical caring of Christians do they listen to the words of the gospel.

"Find a Need and Fill It!"

Yoido Full Gospel Church in Seoul, Korea, is the largest church in the world. It began with four people meeting in a U.S. Army tent that was left behind after the Korean War. Today it has over 700,000 members. One motto of the church is, "Find a need and fill it!"

Yonggi Cho, the founding pastor, encourages members to reach out in practical ways to the needs of those around them with the love of Jesus. You might think that a church that large would be impersonal. The opposite is the case; the church has grown because it emphasizes ministering to the everyday needs of nonbelievers in a personal way.

Did someone just have a baby? Take her a meal. Is someone sick? Visit him in the hospital. Are people discouraged? Listen to them and offer to pray.

Jesus' Love in Action

There are many ways to show Jesus' love to those around us. What are some practical ways you could show His love to those in your sphere of influence?

Here are a few ideas:

- Mowing someone's lawn
- Sending a birthday card
- Baby-sitting
- Taking people a meal or cookies
- Coaching a children's team
- Visiting the hospital
- Pet-sitting
- Helping someone move
- Listening!!!
- Serving
- Allowing someone to serve you

Try one out and see how people respond!

Showing Christ's Friendship

Religious people labeled Jesus as a "Friend of Sinners" (Luke 5:29-32, 7:33-35). They meant it as an insult, but Jesus took it as a compliment.

Everyone needs friends. What are some activities you can participate in with those who do not yet know Christ in order to extend Christ's friendship to them?

Here are a few ideas:

- Having a cookout
- Birthday parties
- Celebrating holidays together
- Having a block party
- "Tupperware" parties
- Hunting together
- Going to a ball game
- Playing cards
- Shopping
- Super Bowl party
- Golfing
- Borrowing (and lending) tools or kitchen supplies
- Etc., Etc., Etc.!

Be open, have fun, and see what God can do in and through these friendships.

Meet People Where They Are

You discovered in the last lesson that influencing people to Christ takes time. Because of this, you can relax and meet people where they are. You don't need to see things happen fast, because different people are usually involved at different points in the process. Remember John 4:37? "One person plants and someone else harvests."

The Response Scale

Growth is more complex than a chart and there are often many ups and downs. But the "Response Scale" helps us realize that people are at different places and we need to meet them where they are and help them grow further with Christ.

> Reproducing Leader
> Growing in Ministry to Others
> Growing in Prayer and Giving
> Actively Sharing Faith
> ▶ Receiving Christ as Lord and Savior
> Considering the Cost of Following Jesus
> Understanding the Gospel
> Genuine Interest in Christian Faith
> Ignorant or Negative Attitude Toward Christ

Seasons of Openness

People are drawn to Christ in different ways—some through meaningful friendships with Christians, some by signs and wonders, and some by intellectual curiosity. Most people, however, are more open to the gospel at times of change or deep need in their lives.

1. Why do you think people are more open to Christ during times of change like those listed below?

- Death in the family
- Injury or Health Problems
- Divorce or Separation
- Job Loss or Change
- Marriage
- Pregnancy, Miscarriage, or Birth
- Financial Trouble
- Relocation

2. If you don't reach out to people in their times of need, what are some destructive sources of help that they might turn to?

Serve!

Look at the names on your Relating Jesus Prayer Card.

1. Write the names of any people on your list that are going through a time of difficulty or change right now.

2. Write down one or two things you can do in the next week to show care or to extend friendship to those individuals.

Share your answers with someone near you, then briefly pray for each other. If at all possible, do one of these things in the coming days. You will share your experiences next time.

Remember to keep praying for those on your prayer card.

Lesson Three – Cooperate

Check In!

Lesson One encouraged you to begin praying consistently for your friends, relatives, and associates who do not yet know Christ. Lesson Two asked you to identify one or two of them and do something concrete to build relationships with them or show them love. How's it going?

- ❏ Wonderful! I am praying and have begun to reach out in practical ways.
- ❏ Good. I am making progress in praying for them and showing them love.
- ❏ Not so good. I have been really busy, but I do intend to begin doing this.
- ❏ To be honest, I am a very selfish person and I don't want to inconvenience myself by praying for and serving others.
- ❏ Other: _____

Share how you are doing with someone else and take a moment to pray for those on your Relating Jesus Prayer Card.

Understand Your Role

Read and discuss the verses below in groups of three or four others:

- "One person plants and someone else harvests" (*Jesus*, John 4:37).
- "My job was to plant the seed in your hearts, and Apollos watered it, but it was God, not we, who made it grow" (*Paul*, 1 Corinthians 3:6).
- "But it is actually best for you that I go away, because if I don't, the Counselor won't come. If I do go away, he will come because I well send him to you. And when he comes, he will convince the world of its sin, and of God's righteousness, and of the coming judgement" (*Jesus*, John 16:7-8).

1. When it comes to sharing your faith, do you see yourself as one who plants, harvests, or waters? Why?

2. What is the Holy Spirit's role in drawing people to Christ?

3. Who were the main people involved in bringing you to Christ and helping you become established in your relationship with Him? What were the different roles that they played in relating Christ to you?

4. What do these verses and your observations say to you about working with others and cooperating with the Holy Spirit as you seek to relate Jesus to new people?

The Power of Teamwork

There are several reasons why introducing non-Christians to more Christians often accelerates their journey to Christ. Here are a few:

- None of us expresses Christ's life completely. The more Christians someone knows, the more fully he or she can see Christ.
- Sometimes there is a Christian friend who has a special rapport with one of our nonbelieving friends because they share a hobby or have been through similar life experiences.
- Nonbelievers often see a special love and commitment in Christians' relationships with each other.
- God can use our diverse gifts to more fully serve our friends.
- A Christian peer group can become an attractive alternative to some people.

Work Together

1. Write down the names of two of your nonbelieving friends, neighbors, co-workers, classmates, or relatives below.

2. Write the names of several Christians who might join you in praying for and loving these individuals.

3. Write down a couple of activities that you might do to build relationships between your believing and nonbelieving friends.

4. Arrange to do at least one of these activities in the next week or two.

Lesson Four – Listen

Any Progress?

The first three lessons of this study encouraged you to love others by praying for them, serving them, and introducing them to other Christians. How are you doing in showing God's love to others?

- ❏ I am making great progress in at least two of the three areas.
- ❏ I'm getting off to a slow start, but I have made definite progress.
- ❏ I'd rather not say how I am doing.
- ❏ Other: _____

Learn to Listen

1. Read Proverbs 18:13 and James 1:19.

2. What do these verses teach you about reaching out to others?

3. How important do you think the skill of caring listening is to sharing Christ?

The Power of Questions

Jesus often used questions, whether it was while teaching, doing ministry, or just everyday life. Questions:

- Help us find out where people are coming from…
- …And keep us from assuming that others are just like us.
- Gauge their level of interest in different areas…
- …And get a sense of our friends' perceived needs.
- Communicate caring empathy…
- …And respect the opinions of others, regardless of whether or not we agree.
- Initiate spiritual conversations…
- …And get others to think critically about life and God.

Connect with People Where They Are

Everyone has different interests and situations in their lives. Let's look at some of the things that draw people together with those they know.

1. Think about a couple of your friends from your list. What do you talk about with them? What do you have in common that makes you want to listen to them?

2. Try to think of a time when a nonbelieving friend was really open about life with you. What started the conversation? What kind of impact did your friendship have on that person?

3. What kind of questions could you ask your friends to simply develop better relationships with them?

Connect with People Spiritually

Here are some useful questions to stimulate spiritual conversations. They begin with simple opening questions and then go deeper. You can mix and match them. You can stop at any point. If someone expresses a genuine interest, you can go deeper. The progression could take five minutes, five weeks, or five years!

Opening Questions
- Are you very interested in spiritual things?
- Where are you in your spiritual journey?
- When have you prayed in your life? Did God answer your prayer?
- If you could design the ideal church, what would it look like?

Probing Questions
- When have you felt God's closeness or help in your life?
- If someone were to ask you, "What is a real Christian?," how would you answer?
- Have you ever personally trusted Christ, or are you still on the way?
- How far along the way are you?

Decision Questions
- Has God proven that he is worthy of your complete trust?
- Do you desire to open your whole life to Jesus?
- Would you like to give your life to Christ now?
- What hinders you from personally trusting Christ?

Remember!
- Be yourself!
- Use a normal vocabulary, not "Christian-ese."
- Don't hide God's goodness. Share what God is doing in your life with your nonbelieving friends just as you would with your small group members.
- If people are interested, they can ask you questions.
- Trust the Holy Spirit to guide you.

What's Next?

1. How do you want to grow in reaching out to others? Check all that apply.

    ❏ Actively pray for others
    ❏ Learn to listen
    ❏ Clear my schedule so I have time for relationships
    ❏ Serve others with simple acts of kindness
    ❏ Introduce my Christian and non-Christian friends to one another
    ❏ Make my words "accessible" to non-Christians
    ❏ Hear what God wants to do in my relationships
    ❏ Ask God to help me really love people again

2. What is one simple action you can do this week to reach out to others?

3. What is one simple question you can ask to get to know someone better this week?

Extra Credit

Use one or several questions given in this lesson (or some of your own) to explore where your friends, relatives, or associates are in their spiritual journeys.

Lesson Five – Share

What's Happening?

What's happening with your friends, so far?

- ❏ It seems like good stuff is happening.
- ❏ I think some things are happening, but I can't really tell for sure.
- ❏ I find myself asking, "Why is God taking a nap?"
- ❏ Huh? Oh, sorry. I just woke up.
- ❏ Other: _____

What efforts have you made that have worked? Has anything flopped miserably? Failures are okay, too. The important thing is that you are trying. Share as a group.

Are You Ready?

"If you are asked about your Christian hope, always be ready to explain it. But you must do this in a gentle and respectful way" (1 Peter 3:15-16).

"Live wisely among those who are not Christians, and make the most of every opportunity. Let your conversation be gracious and effective so that you will have the right answer for everyone" (Colossians 4:5-6).

1. How do the two passages above speak to you about sharing Christ with others?

2. How ready do you feel to share what Christ means to you with someone who doesn't yet know Him?

   ❏ Very prepared
   ❏ Somewhat prepared
   ❏ Unprepared
   ❏ Very unprepared
   ❏ Other: _____

Talking

1. Have you ever had a time where someone was talking to you, and you were clueless about what he or she was trying to say? What was the experience like?

2. How can you make your language more clear and accessible when you discuss spiritual matters?

Answering Questions

Last week, you talked about asking questions. Some of you may have noticed people asking *you* questions in the past week. Here are some thoughts on answering questions.

- Be clear. Make sure you are answering the question asked. You both may end up confused if you answer questions that a person doesn't need answered.
- Be gentle. Mercy is God's method. If you are overly harsh in your response, you may end up hurting your friends.
- Be accurate. If you're not sure of the answer, don't fake it. Do some research if you need to!
- Be honest. Ultimately, reality is your friend. Let kindness and truth be your guide.

Above all, remember that you don't have to be perfect. You are learning, and you are learning with everyone in the group.

The Power of Your Personal Story

Sharing a personal testimony often communicates powerfully to others because...

- It is personal and from the heart.
- You have credibility with your audience.
- No one can deny its reality.
- It's non-threatening.
- It can be adapted to each individual's felt needs.

A simple pattern for sharing your personal story comes from Paul's testimony in Acts 26:9-23. It is sometimes called the "BEST" pattern because of its four parts:

> **B**efore you received Christ
> **E**vents leading up to your salvation
> **S**alvation day
> **T**oday—God's work in your life now

Some people have stories more like Timothy's than Paul's. If you accepted Christ at a very early age, you can start with the "S" in the "BEST" pattern.

Practice Sharing a Two-Minute Testimony

Write several phrases under each section:

B—Before you received Christ as your Lord and Savior.
- What were key factors in your life before Christ?
- Build bridges and establish common ground with your listener.
- Don't share disgusting details or glory in past sins.

E—Events leading up to your salvation.
- What events or circumstances led up to your receiving Christ?
- Trace God's work in the journey. He is the center of your testimony, not you.
- Emphasize one key principle or problem (lack of peace, pride, emptiness, etc.) and how it effected your everyday life.
- Share your fears or thoughts.
- Share something good about your life that others can relate to (i.e., generosity, honesty, etc.).

S—Salvation day.
- Focus on Christ–His love and provision.
- What thoughts went through your mind?
- How did it happen?
- Specifically tell how you received Christ so that the individual will know how when he or she chooses to.
- Avoid religious jargon.

T—Today
- How did Christ change your life?
- Show how He dealt with fears or problems you mentioned earlier.
- Focus on the most striking change.
- Be honest—Christ has changed you but still has a lot of work to do!
- Share your excitement for something God is doing in your life right now.

You may have practiced your testimony before, but practice makes perfect, right? So practice sharing your story with one other person right now. Try to do it in two minutes or less. Ready...Set...Go!

Stepping Out

1. What do you think your story might mean for people?

2. What is the next step for you this week?

3. On a scale of 1 to 10, from feeling useless (1) to bubbling with Jesus (10), how do you feel about your progress in *Relating Jesus* to others? Share with a friend and pray for your continued growth and new opportunities.

Lesson Six – Invite

How's It Going?

Over the past month or so, you have been encouraged to put Jesus' love for others into action by praying, serving, cooperating with others, listening to the nonbelievers around you, and sharing God's work in your life. Do you feel like you are learning and changing? Do you have experiences or things to share?

Check Your Attitude

1. Read Luke 15:1-7. Jesus and the Pharisees saw "sinners" very differently. Their differences in attitude went back to how they saw God. To express this difference, Jesus told three stories.

2. On the attitude scale below, put a "P" where you think the Pharisees' concept of God fell. Place a "J" where you think Jesus' was. Then place an "X" to mark where your own gut-level concept of God is right now.

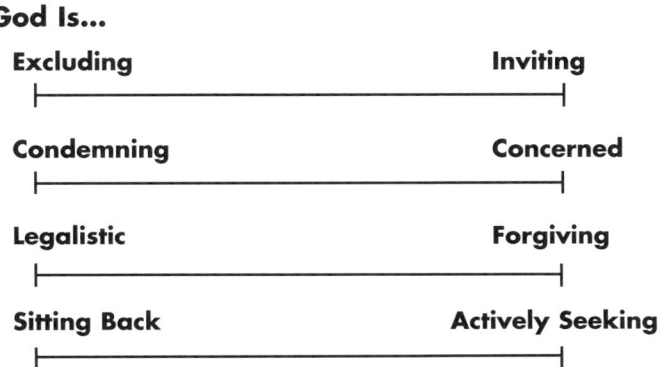

Invite!

Relating Jesus to others begins by inviting them into our lives. Jesus invited people to join him in what he did, no matter what it looked like to others. Love means meeting people where they are. Take a chance; invite people into your life.

Invite Small

1. What events or activities could your small group plan that would be inviting to nonbelievers?

2. Who could you invite that would be interested in these events?

3. What things are your friends doing that you might be interested in trying out?

4. What other friends do you have that might be interested in doing these same things?

Invite BIG

1. What events or activities of your church could you invite nonbelievers to where they could build relationships with Christians and/or hear a clear gospel message? Write current or new possibilities below.

2. Are there special events coming up (like Christian concerts or plays) in your community or in nearby churches that are well done and clearly present a Christian message?

3. What special groups or classes are you aware of that offer the hope and power of Christ to the questions, needs or hurts of nonbelievers? (i.e., ALPHA, divorce seminars, grief groups, recovery groups, marriage workshops, parenting classes, etc.)

4. What friends, relatives, neighbors, or associates of yours might be open to an invitation in the coming weeks or months?

5. What do you need from this group to continue to grow in reaching out to others?

Say It Again

In Lesson One, you were asked how many times you heard the good news of Christ before you truly said "yes" to Him. Most people need to hear the message several times before they receive Christ.

1. Why do you think this is true?

2. If you unrealistically expect people to accept Christ the very first time you share your testimony with them, or if you bring them to church and they don't respond, what might you conclude? Check any conclusions that you personally might make.

   ❏ This person is closed to the gospel.
   ❏ I did or said something wrong.
   ❏ He or she was not listening.
   ❏ I'm not going to invite this person again.
   ❏ The principles in the *Relating Jesus* book don't work for me.
   ❏ Other thought(s): _____

3. Think about it…Where would you be right now if others had given up on you as spiritually unreceptive after the first time you heard the message of Christ?

Most people need time and multiple exposures to the gospel to process the life-changing decision to follow Christ. Because of that, you should offer others many opportunities to hear the good news of Christ.

Parting Words

1. So how do you feel now about *Relating Jesus*? Better? Worse?

2. How would you rate your progress as you've been taking the course? Put an "X" where you were and a circle where you are now.

	Apathetic	**Engaged**
Praying	├--┤	
Serving	├--┤	
Cooperating	├--┤	
Listening	├--┤	
Sharing	├--┤	
Inviting	├--┤	

3. What do you think is the greatest insight you have received during this course?

4. How do you want to reach out to those on your prayer card in the weeks and months ahead?

5. Close in prayer.

Notes

Notes

Notes